TECHNOLOGY
BYTES BACK

MESSAGES FROM THE FONTLINE
OF THE COMPUTER REVOLUTION

www.wessex.media

First Published in 2018 by Wessex Media
9 Dibdin View, Bridport, Dorset. DT6 5FA

10 9 8 7 6 5 4 3 2 1

British Library Cataloguing in Publication Data
A catalogue record is available on request
from the British Library

ISBN 978-1-9164278-0-8

Photography, cover design, lay out
and page setting by Wessex Media

Printed and bound by
Cylex, 21 Old Street, Bailie Gate Industrial Estate
Sturminster Marshall, Dorset, BH21 4DB

ACKNOWLEDGEMENTS

I would like to thank the following organisations and publications in which some poems in this collection have been either published or performed. I am grateful for your support and encouragement over the years. Apothecary, Bridport; Story Traders Bridport; Writers in the Alley Dorchester; Black Ven South-West; Vittles and Verse Lyme Regis; Apples and Snakes South West; Hammer and Tongue South; Word Makers Silence Breakers Bournemouth; The TeaPoet Collective Romsey; The Rainbow Fish Speak Easy Yeovil; The Hip Yak Poetry Shack; Taking The Mic Exeter; Dorset Writers Network; The Yeovil Literary Prize; I Am Not A Silent Poet; The Ampersand; and The Western Gazette.

Thank you in particular to my endlessly patient wife Indigo and my mother-in-law Gill Fifield who got me writing again. To my mum and my dad. Special thanks to my brother David Roe and my friend Tom Rogers. Also to my Professor Mavis Donner-Bonney who lit the fire. To my friends and family who have lent me willing ears over the last few years and given so much encouragement, support and positive energy and helped me make it this far... Ged Duncan, Rob Casey, Sarah Acton, Louisa Adjoa Parker, Michael Forte, Miriam San Marco, Damian O'Vitch, Danielle Gontier and big, big kudos to Laura Johnson and Syd Meats, my very own grammar thugs!

For Amy, Arthur and Robin

CONTENTS

Foreword

I bunked off school at age twelve to watch a crane install a computer through the roof of a local hauliers. Two years later, in Computer Studies we were still learning about punchcards and ticker tape. But 1977 was a year of change. The first microprocessor computer I actually touched was nothing more than a circuit board and processor. When one of the other kids managed to make it smoke by giving it a 'divide by zero' command I was hooked. Ever since I have had an unending attraction to all things technological.

So at sixteen I did a brief stint as a lab technician before joining the Air Force in Air Traffic Control. This brought me into contact with computers in the workplace and this amazing contraption the size of a wardrobe called a MuFax. We used to have to test it everyday but you could send an A4 page of words, a photo or a diagram in something less than newspaper quality but it took up to ten minutes. It was mostly 'tested' with funny drawings or inspirational quotes, I think these were the early memes of our military network.

We also used a computer system for other purposes but on the overnight shifts we sometimes chatted with other operators at bases in Scotland. This was by means of a simple line of text typed into the bottom of the screen and their reply was displayed at the top. This was the nineteen eighties, I am not sure it was even stored anywhere but it was an early prelude to things like instant messengers.

Concurrent with this there was a home micro revolution and Sir Clive Sinclair brought us the ZX81 and The Spectrum. I remember a crowd of us around a 16k ZX81 playing Football Manager. Every so often one of us would go off to perform his guard duty or other task but we would always come straight back to have one more go! The Cold War wasn't quite so hot anymore but that would have been a good summer for the Russians to invade!

I taught myself Basic and then took a couple of RAF computer courses. I came out of the Air Force and managed to get a place on a TOPS computer training course in Manchester. I learnt about boring business languages like COBOL and RPG2. Actually the whole school algebra thing suddenly made sense. Now I knew how to apply it in the real world.

So jobs came and went but my one constant was computers. As a hobbyist and as an operator, implementer and champion. Through vocational computer courses over the years I finally found myself applying my knowledge as web designer, a trainer and network manager at a university in The Netherlands. Whilst working there just before the millennium turned over, I started a degree in Computing and Media and one of my elective courses was Poetry. Something I had played with for years but my professor lit a fire under me. I was revisiting old stuff, rewriting, creating and renewing my passion for poetry and writing.

I shared a chapbook of my poems with my father and he said I reminded him of Ogden Nash. "Who's Ogden Nash?" I said. Later I went off to the bookstore and found a suitable volume and this interchange with my father was the trigger that started a real War of Words. An exchange of poetastery where rapid fire poems were exchanged through email that dragged many of my siblings into a Poetry War! As the words flew it created a schism within the family. 'The War of The Words' that followed was a breeding ground for my early performance pieces. What did I write about? Things that amused or inspired me, technology, peoples relationships with computers, the internet and random stuff.

Someone recently asked me "How long have you been writing?" I smiled and replied, "Since I was about four…" The truth is I was playing with the limerick form when I was eight or nine because I loved Edward Lear's Nonsense Poems and I have since used it as an approachable form for workshops of primary age kids. I wrote my first haiku at secondary school and the subject was the electricity pylons marching across the countryside. I realised that there were rules to poetry and this suited a young boy trying to find a niche to fit into.

As an adult I was finally diagnosed with Aspergers and ADHD and it was if I had been playing football without knowing the rules Things were suddenly clear, and I knew where the goalposts were! Some of these things have informed my choice of subjects but I have always had a passion for poems and technology and hopefully I managed to light some fires of my own along the way. This selection is a glimpse inside my head and I hope it surprises some of those people who only ever knew me as 'The Computer Geek' who came to sort out their computer problems.

Peter Roe
September 2018

The March of Progress

Trilobites to bits and bytes
Megaliths to megabits
Ammonites to gigabytes
This is the march of progress

Interaction and implementation
Integration of information
Opt out of natural progression
View the genome for your selection
This is the new religion
This is the march of progress

Seeking a friend with good vibration?
This is about binary attraction
This is on-line fornication
Click through for your selection...
This is the new religion
This is the march of progress

Seeking God or soul redemption?
Want to confess for absolution?
Food for the soul or confirmation?
Or just an excommunication!
This is the new religion
This is the march of progress

Interaction and Implementation
Integration of Information
The human race can interface
This is the internet
This is the new religion
This is the march of progress

Hard Driving

I am the Techno-Shaman

I live in a Haych-Tee Tee-Pee

I got myself a dotcom internet Address

I got myself some of that Eee-mail

I got myself an Eye-Ess-Pee

With loads of Kay-Bee-Pease

I'm rammed up, I'm turned on, I'm high on Ee

I'm hard driving on the information super highway

Cruising for a link

A HOT HOT You-Are-ELL

My Eye-Ess-Dee-En is running hot

My Pee-See-Eye can really fly

My hardware's hard

and my software's NOT

I got myself a dotcom internet Address

I got myself some of that Eee-mail

Ee-chat, Ee-Commerce, Eye-See-Queue

I'm *'virtually'* yours

I'm rammed up, I'm turned on, I'm high on Ee

I'm Hard driving, cruising on the information super-highway

Spam's Off!

I seem to remember, when I was a lad
Sitting in a caf' with me dear old dad
and fag ash Lil with her face so hard
slouched on over and gave us a card

Covered in stains from the greasy food
and an attitude that bordered on being bloody rude
She'd get out a pencil and her little notebook
She'd scratch her nose and give you that look

That says "I'm busy, I haven't got all day"
Then she opens her mouth and what does she say?
"You can't have breakfast it's long past ten"
So we look at the card to start choosing again

"Ketchup is extra and we haven't any hake...
and you'll have to wait 'cos cooks on his break"
She interrupts herself with a delicate cough
"Oh and by the way... the spam's off!"

Miss Information

I was surfing on the internet like I usually do...
A window popped up "A Message For You!"
I clicked on the button with some trepidation
It opened right up an E-mail communication

It's a message from you saying "Hello it's me
please message me back and then we shall see
if we can have an affair in a meaningful way
or should we stop it right now and call it a day"

I stop what I'm doing and think for a while
Then start to write and begin with a smile
You know what I mean... a little emoticon
that signifies a mood or a hat you have on

:o)

I send an e-mail back with kindest salutations
and a quick-fire answer to your hot propositions
Just check your recipients before you click send
to direct mail to your lover and not to your friend!

The Digital Frontier - Bullshit Two Point Zero

We get our news in headlines and trending quotes
Despotic Tyrants hack computers to sway our votes
Egomaniacs trump their worth from their ivory towers
Politicians line their pockets with money that is ours
Whilst the fat cat bankers and the Global Corporation
Ruin our economies and sell our personal information

It seems the *Arab Spring* has sprung and broken
And Twits and Tweets though loud and outspoken
Have failed to cast an illuminating light
On the refugees and their desperate plight

But we all did our bit, clicked and ticked and joined a group
That added our opinion and thoughts to the digital soup
So is technology backing a new wave of Cyber-Activation?
Is this really People Power... or just Human Corporatisation?

The World's Gone Digital But My Mum's Still Analog

We have entered a new age of digital information

That demands our time and unlimited interaction

Our smartphones with all their chirping and squawking

Have us clicking and ticking and tweeting and talking

Our personal information, our words and our thoughts

Are sent through technology as ones and as noughts

And our social calendar is not defined any more

By an impromptu, but analog, knock on the door

The world may have gone and caught the digital bug

But my arms are still analog and my mum needs a hug

The Dot Com Story

(Sing to the tune of Richard Corey)
With apologies to Simon and Garfunkel and Edward Arlington Robinson!

They say the dot COM stories own one half of the Dow Jones
With Internet connections to spread the word around
Log in to wired society, surf, shop online
You can buy all-a-man can want, music, books and style

But why... A dot COM story
'Cos I curse the life I'm living
'Cos I curse my poverty
And I wish that I could be,
Oh, I wish that I could be,
Oh, I wish that I could be
A dot COM story.

The pundits rave about the stocks most everywhere you go
Dot COM stories on the TV, Dot COM story at a show
And the rumours of the mergers raise the prices quite a lot
The brokers must be happy with everything they've got

But why... A dot COM story
'Cos I curse the life I'm living
'Cos I curse my poverty
And I wish that I could be,
Oh, I wish that I could be,
Oh, I wish that I could be
A dot COM story.

Surf freely, give to charity, have sex without the touch,
Sites are grateful for your patronage for clicks, and views and
such
Their minds will blow asunder when they hear the news just said
Dot COM stories shares crashed last night...
so Internet stocks are dead

Clickbait

One Hundred things to do before you're dead
Seventy Five objects impaled in someone's head
Fifty celebrities that married too young
Twenty Five songs that shouldn't be sung
Twenty things for surprising your cats
Fifteen ways to be eating less fats
Ten most unexpected Darwin Awards
Nine different fruits cut by swords
Eight surprising photos that will be banned
Seven politicians whose careers got canned
Six crazy pranks carried out for a bet
Five stupid things you'll probably regret
Four different reasons not to click on a link
Three more windows so you don't have to think
Two more mistakes and you'll get the sack
One more hour that you won't be getting back
Why is it... that we are all so easily led
By a promise of cats in an online thread
A saccharine solution of kittens and tweets
Smartphone warfare or crushing of sweets
Or by the prospect of riches without any strings
Promised by the tech of the internet of things
We respond to the posts from our digital friends
In a real time sharing that goes on without ends
Don't click with your mouse you know it's a trap
To persuade the unwary to buy lots of crap
When is our attention not wanted any more
Perhaps it's when death is knocking at the door
"One Hundred things to do before you are dead?"
Turn off your devices and try living instead

Memory Buffer Full

There isn't half some rubbish goes flowing through my mind
If a doctor could examine it I wonder what she'd find?
I really wish I could channel it, try to make things better
Or even sit upon a chair and write my Mum a letter

The taps are always open it's like an endless flow
everything gets washed away and my ideas never grow
I tried hard to stop and meditate, like that Buddha fellow
But I didn't reach Nirvana and it only made me mellow

Technology isn't helping my message box is full
I'm gonna change my identity and go and live in Hull
Or maybe California where they say the living is easy
or up on top a mountain where the wind is nice and breezy

That at least would clear my head and help me concentrate
But then I'd miss those little chats and coffee with my mate
Perhaps I need some time to think and clear my mental bin
Then with all that space I make, I could fit more rubbish in

Tilting at Windmills

I wrote a poem about Max Gate
on my smartphone, my digital mate
Over the weeks I added more
but still I wasn't quite sure
if I could ever really dare
to put my name on a poem out there
Linked with Hardy and his home
To be included in my poetic tome

The words were good, the words were mine
Perhaps I needed a little more time
To reflect, to polish, to hone my skill
before tilting at this particular windmill

So I shut it down and put it away
meaning to continue on another day
Then it happened I lost my phone
and that particular digital poem

I had a dream and wrote it fast
about a journey in my past
That started, but was incomplete
and this dream knocked me off my feet

The poem about Hardy or so it seems
had come to me in lucid dreams
It was my unfinished journey all over again
so I got out my smartphone… my digital pen

I searched at length for my missing file
I hadn't looked in quite some while
and I really hoped that I would find
that errant poem from my mind...

But the poem was lost deleted, gone
so I had no means to carry on
I had to start again from scratch
to try and make the words that match
The poetic stanza that was in my head
but the inspiration had long since fled
and so no matter what I tried to say
I couldn't make the words bend my way

Despite my years and supposed sense
sitting up there on my digital fence
dispensing my advice on digital data
about backups and saving for later
It seems I hadn't backed up my stuff
That version on my phone was not enough
So take some advice and make me proud
and back up your data... in the cloud

TMI - Too Much Information

The internet is filled with traps for the unwary
It's overflowing with stuff that is verging on scary
We should block it and save our innocent youth
And try to protect them from the horrible truth
The internet is dangerous and full of rabbit holes
With films about cats that suck on our souls
You'll be exposed to facts, celebrity and fame
And to strange concepts that will stick in your brain

It will fill your mind up with ideas and with thoughts
Delivered to your devices as ones and as noughts
It will affect your opinions in many strange ways
In multi threaded arguments that go on for days
It could compromise your safety and general health
It could affect your home and even your wealth
It's best to stay away from the World Wide Web
Otherwise you'll become really well read

You'll be exposed to people that actually think
And when you find yourself standing at the brink
It's too late, you've developed a habit for thinking
You could have been at the pub gradually drinking
Yourself toward an actual liver cirrhosis
Instead you've been learning by digital osmosis
And now your grey matter is constantly churning
With all that knowledge you've been gradually learning

And you know what's worse? Information will kill
Or at the very least knowledge will make you ill
Ask a cyber-chondriac how she is feeling
That question alone will put her stress through the ceiling
Stay off the internet and give yourself a chance
Try to live out your life in blissful ignorance
Soaking up information is so much worse my friends
Because it seems that thinking will hasten your ends

Einstein, Aristotle, Da Vinci, Faraday and Plato
Tesla, Spinoza, Newton, Hawking and Michelangelo
The worlds greatest thinkers the most well read
Have one thing in common… Every one of them's dead

Information Overload

I've got a Pee Cee with a broad band contraption,
that gives me the internet and network interaction.
And a Four Kay Tee Vee with digital information,
that dishes up soap using it's satellite connection.

I'm integrated and interfaced and wired to the hilt.
I get all the gadgets just as soon as they're built.
I'm hip and I'm cool and I'm trying not to get old,
but really I'm approaching information overload...

I got myself a smart phone to keep me connected
and an alarm for the house to keep me protected.
And microchips for my cats to keep them located
and an Ex Bone for my kids to keep them placated

I'm integrated and interfaced and wired to the hilt.
I get all the gadgets just as soon as they're built.
I'm hip and I'm cool and I'm trying not to get old,
but really I'm approaching information overload...

I'm targeted with adverts from morning till night.
"Hey buy this for a dollar!" or "Buy this cheap flight!"
or its "Pick me ups" and "Niagra" and "Hot Totty" too
or "A Cruising Holiday" or "A Day Trip to the Zoo!"

I integrated and interfaced with digital communication
but all the gadgets gave me was information saturation
I'm not hip and not cool and I'm starting to feel old
and I think I've finally reached information overload

Why Don't You Like Me?

According to the algorithm
You are just my type
You lean to the left of centre
And ignore the usual hype

I left a picture on my page
Of a cute and fluffy cat
I thought that that would do it
But no… You didn't like that

I added a little comment
At the bottom of your post
I was certain it would amuse you
But I was not who you liked most

Maybe I don't attract you
Perhaps it's just my eyes
Is it my lack of fashion?
Or maybe it's just my size

Or is it my profile photo?
Is my hair a bit too long?
Oh why don't you like me?
Please tell me what's wrong

I have posted a photo of puppies
I know that everyone likes that
I dissed some chavs and yuppies
I thought it would make you react

But there was no favourable reaction
So I guess you didn't like that
I am going to end this interaction
And be myself… Oh… You liked that!

Data Fix

Wireless and broadband, fibre to your home
The newest fastest smartphone with the right to roam
Dispensing social media in lots of little doses
Get your fixes from a pharmacy that never closes

On demand and streaming right into your home
A line of digital data pushed out to your phone
This digital lobotomy for the working classes
Is a social band aid, panacea for the masses

The problem for the people, folk like you and me
We are impaled on the horns of a digital dichotomy
We want it, we need it, where do we begin?
The more that we use it the more it sucks us in!

The Confessional Booth

I wait patiently, my first client of the day?
A man no youth… shuffles to the adjacent booth…
He coughs and grunts, says nothing, goes away.

A young woman enters. Carrying a heavy load?
Her desperate moans for help, full of dark overtones
I channel her call into the ether… Switch to "God" Mode?

She gets her answer, a measure of absolution…
Her face lifts, a smile, happy now, for a while…
Past the waiting queue, acolytes to communication

A fat cigar smoking man, sees her face that smiles
He smiles back, winks… I am God's gift he thinks
She steps back, recoils, for he is what she most reviles

He epitomises sloth and gluttony, a capitalistic pig
So fat on lions shares. Gives pennies to charity… cares?
Almost too large to fit inside, this 'self-made' man Mr Big?

This *Dow Jones* talks about playing *Footsie* with *Nikki*
Indulgent sexual(?) conquests, highs… lows… bequests?
For the other waiting petitioners I interrupt, I take pity

Voice both soft and commanding. With my ritualistic phrase
Guaranteed to stop them all, in the middle of the call
"Deposit twenty pence for the next three minutes, Please…"

The Burning Bush

"A miracle bush that burns without leaving ash...
Carbon dating shows Turin Shroud is a fake...
Five Britons die in biggest ever Air Crash...
All that and more coming up after this break..."

"Eight out of ten owners say they prefer it..."
"Summer holiday bonus, we'll help you pack..."
"A new exhaust for your car at Quick-ee-fit..."
"Now our eye witness news... Welcome Back..."

"When we arrived it was firmly ablaze
As we got out the hose. It went out
There was the bush wearing smoke haze
It wasn't even singed, see why we doubt."

"It was once in a lifetime combination
Of weather phenomenon. No doubt
Statistical data will give confirmation
That proves it burnt and went out."

"We came around that corner there
And the whole bush was on fire
Some stupid hiker who didn't care
Incurring the Forest Ranger's ire."

"It was the first great miracle
A sign sent by God for a man
A bush that burned... Incredible..."
"An eye witness there, Mr Abraham...

Next those other stories after this message..."

The War of The Words

When two brothers argued and insults went forth
They agreed to separate to the South and the North
They had no more contact for years at a time
And when they did speak it was only in rhyme

For they both had discovered a talent for verse
And as hobbies go it could have been worse
Pete was in the south... a technology junkie
He fixed computers, a kind of network monkey

Dave he went North he was the manual type
An 'Unexpected Poet' if you believe all the hype
And between his gigs what he did for a job
Was sweeping of chimneys or carrying a hod

But there was no love lost between Dave and his brother
Despite an intervention from their sister and mother
Fate had brought the brothers to the same destination
It was a Poetry Competition with a ladder elimination

Poet would play Poet and the names were drawn out
With names preselected to sort the matched bout
Pete looked at the board and by the luck of the draw
He was matched against someone he'd not met before

The rounds they went quickly and each poet passed
led up to the final... where they might meet at last
The chances were slim that they would fight one another
But it finally happened... it was brother on brother

The air was spread thick with a cacophony of rhyme
Sonnets, Limericks and *odes* but I don't have the time
To read you the *Wakas,* the *Tankas* or the *Canto*
the *Paradelle,* the *Madrigal* or lilting *Rispetto*

There was *Assonance* and *Dissonance, Meter* and *Verse*
Strophes and *Antistrophes, Allusion* and much worse...
The words spilled out going backwards and forth
But neither gave way not The South or The North

Pete used a *Villanelle* and caught David off guard
Then followed with *enjambment* that is reputedly hard
to use it quite well in a poem and in a believable way
but he seemed to pull it off on this momentous day!

Dave winced and cringed... "you damned fool you!"
He opened his book and whipped out a quick *Haiku*
And the words that flowed in his mellifluous voice
Had Pete weeping in shame but it left him no choice

He dredged through his memory for dirty *Poetastery*
and whipped out his *Doggerel* both pointed and nasty
He caught his brother off guard hit him hard in the seat
with a *Dactyl...* and with a *Dimeter* two *Metrical Feet*

But his moment of victory was fleeting and *Pyrrhic*
As the rapid riposte was both magic and mythic
Dave's *iambic Pentameter* walked all over his brother
and left him in pieces shouting out for his mother

But Pete he bounced back... like a piece of elastic
Knowing his next one would be something quite drastic
He called up a *hexameter*, thats the one with six feet
An *Allegorical Anachronism* it was really quite sweet

But Dave saw it coming and with a duck of the head
He dodged the *hexameter*, firing a *heptameter* instead
It was an *epigram* from a *Ballad* of *Epic* proportion
For use in an emergency... and only with caution!

Pete was hit by the *heptameter* it caught him full force
He knew that he was cornered but he had no recourse
So he rifled his memory for *Abstract* or *Found Verse*
Because he knew in his heart this would only get worse

But Dave stepped back and took a short breath
For he knew that this slam was a duel to the death
His conscience was pricked and he didn't quite dare
So he fired two *Quatrains*, straight up in the air

And Pete had been preparing a *Didactic Epitaph*
Instead he shrugged it off with a wave and a laugh
Both brothers had realised this poetry convention
Could only end in Mutually Assured Collaboration

So the brothers they stood, shoulder to shoulder
To try something new, much brighter, much bolder
Their *Two Voice Poem* got the audience to their feet
And the Poetry Slam? …was declared a Dead Heat.

Metro Tango

I watch her reflection in the window
Houses pass behind her face
Our eyes dance away for a while
She smiles a smile, an almost smile

Our eyes accidentally touch
My heart skips a beat
Her foot moves, it catches my leg
I thrill. More… With my eyes I beg

She turns to say something… Stops
My heart thumps in anticipation
Our eyes together for a moment sharing
Subliminal messages, daring... Daring…

Dancing with our eyes
A tango in a public place
A secret no one sees, no one shares
An act that neither she nor I quite dares…

A final glance… A bow of the head
Unrequited passion, a silent goodbye
She steps to her door, I step to mine
Strangers dancing in metro-nomic time

Catching The Morning Rush

That point when darkness departs and daylight demands
I dream of you
The soft anticipation of our quiet time together
I think of you
That moment when I leave the bed
When I feel the cold morning air on my body
I desire you

My eyes slowly slough the skin of sandy sleep
I want you
That clicking sound you make as you leap from the sack
I hear you
The harsh growl of the machine
When I prepare you for your morning bath
I desire you

The sibilant susseration of the scalding water
I lust for you
The subtle aroma of your heavenly body
I smell you
Those minutes while you soak
Those subtle perfumes of yours wash over me
I desire you

A presumptive ping from the micro-wave oven
I forget you
But only for a second, then my attention is yours
I return to you

I stroke your golden body

Small circles with the back of a silver spoon

I desire our union

I long for your warm touch on my lips

I must have you

I reach for you, touch your warm vessel

I anticipate

I pull you toward me, inhaling

I tip you forward and swallow your golden fluid

Kenya Gold I love you

- Ode to coffee beans

The Birth of Chimera

No choice or steps can prevent
The birth of a dragon from hell
A lottery of chance that fate has sent
Conceived in a hidden cell

His silent attack that never fails
His tail of plates around your heart
His rapid growth of deadly scales
That sharpest knives can't slice apart

Feed yourself with free radicals
Bombard him with your radiation
Align yourself with new age fanaticals
Fight for life for your salvation
Drink down chemical weapon cocktails
Pray to your Gods if all else fails

Thinfluence

To all my thin friends who say they're a mate

Who can eat and can eat without gaining weight

Who point to the internet and various books

That offer ways to diet with celebrity cooks

Offering supplemental vitamins methods and herbs

Organic, sustainable, beansprouts and curds

Paleo, vegan, smoothies and acacia berry

With trendy names like "*Eat, Shrink and be Merry*"

and *"Thinfluence"*. "*Aztec*", "*Zen*" and "*Neanderthin*"

"*Quantum Eating*" or "*Eating chocolate without Sin*"

Then there's "*Feed your Brain Lose Your Belly*"

I think my wife saw that one on the Telly

So ditch the potatoes and eat lots of rice

Drop all of the bad stuff... Thats 'anything nice'

Cos when your body is craving a nice tasty snack

They're loaded with sugar to make you come back

Try fasting and feasting for days at a time

Try following a diet of seaweed and slime

Try a detox and an enema, or going without

Try drinking just water till nothing comes out

If you do all of this stuff and you're still left alive

You'll find that you weigh only seven stone five

Delicate Essence

I am waiting my turn in the sandwich line
I've got my mind set on something quite fine
Trying to decide if I should go whole grain
or something with fish for feeding the brain.

Do I go for the barm cake or the big doughy bun?
Some cheese on a teacake? Something quite fun.
Or coronation chicken with salad on the edge…
Or a floury bloomer with mozzarella and veg.

Maybe a foot long sub with bacon and egg inside…
or something else all together I cant quite decide.
I'm watching her work, she catches my eye…
She holds up an offering "Pastrami on Rye"

The customer goes off clutching his prize…
"Your turn is coming…" promise her eyes.
There are four more in line in front of me
One gets his falafel and then there are three

The egg mayo salad is done in record time.
Two more to go and then she'll be mine…
"Cream cheese and pineapple on a granary bun"
Is quickly despatched and then there is one.

He asks for a potato with beef chilli stew
and while I am waiting, for the potato to do.
The door comes open and two punters come in
So I step to the back and start waiting again.

She neatly despatches a tuna salad bun
adds a drink and a cake and then he is gone
And finally its done, the last customer steps up
Its a bacon butty with both mayo and ketchup

He picks up some crisps… and a fizzy drink
And on his way out, he gives a big wink…
She heads for the door and on the way past
she says "Thank goodness we're alone at last"

As the door starts to close I mentally undress
This fine sandwich maker this Goddess of Cress
When she flips the sign from open to shut
My attention wanders at the sight of her…

And then the sound of the key closing the lock
Brings me right back and I start to take stock
Of this delectable delicacy wearing a net hat
She smiles… "would sir like undressing with that?"

Get Your Rocks Off!

While out walking the dog on the local sands
The wife found a rock that needed two hands
To pick it up, she duly did and carried it home
To identify that chunk in a rock spotters tome

Encrusted on the rock were crystals bright
On a first glance perhaps... Blue Azurite
The rock beneath was covered with salt
Quite dense and black maybe it was basalt

This conclusion though, did not sit so well
With the geological map that the shops do sell
Samples were chipped and photos were snapped
Then sent to the folk who had previously mapped

The whole of the British Geological Strata
to see if they were maybe a little smarter
than the wife and I who by now could not agree
on that damn rock's classification or pedigree.

After all our local avenues were exhausted
"Take me to the museum" my wife exhorted.
So to the museum we carried her rocks off
So that the experts could poke and scoff

And some weeks later we had a telephone call
That indicated a verdict had been reached by all
So we went right away to see the museum folk
We were met at the door by the rock expert bloke

With a knowing smile he handed my wife the bag
Just spoke right out and said "North East Slag!"
I said "Hang on a minute you Southern ponce…
You can't know that you've only met her once!"

"Apart from anything else you stupid bloke…
She's from the South, born in Basingstoke!"
"Oh, no, no, no" he said "you misunderstand"
"It's industrial slag from up in yon Geordieland…"

"Oh" said I suddenly feeling quite better
"You mean blast furnace melt and spetter!"
"Yes he said some time ago it came to be
a 19th century ship would have gone to sea

With waste like this in the bottom of the boat
to give it ballast… so it would upright float
In order to take cargo to maximise their scoff
they'd dump the slag.. and then make off"

"Right" says I "I think it's now quite clear
how yon Geordie Slag came to be laying here
It seems that this practice went on a lot
of fly tipping their slag in our beauty spot"

"Its a fact that they cared little for our beaches
Those capitalistic blood sucking Geordie leeches
So visitors take note when you come sailing in
Take your rubbish home or just use the bin!"

Mary Anning

She sold sea shells on the sea shore
I am sure you heard that rhyme before
To academia there was nothing quite as frightening
As this Clever Little Woman... struck by lightening

And though they used her ill she made no claims
Upon the men of learning who sucked her brains
Of the knowledge she gleaned from the sea shore
About the petrified beasts from the times before

On her fossil fish, invertebrates and so much more
All those learned gentlemen's careers did soar
And though well spoken and known so well
She lived upon the fossils that she could sell

I think it is this poor woman's God given right
To be remembered for more than just copralite
So when you are out on the beaches scanning
Think on... and give thanks to our Mary Anning

The Cobb

Her harbour huddled hard against the shoreline
Unyielding she stands, a squat, silent bastion
Defiant against the footfall of her chain of visitors
Angus, Barbara, Connor, Doris, Ewan...
All are frustrated by her stubborn watch
She stands resolute, a serpent of stone
Awash in the spittle of her angry tormentors
Protecting her charges from the wrath of the storms

Platty-tudes

I know that I shouldn't make a fuss
But there is no plural for Platypus
This patchwork creature, genus *Monotremes*
Is an egg laying mammal... or so it seems
Is it any wonder the male is venomous
For he has no plurals like we, them 'n us
No Platty Pussies, Pusses or Plattypi
He is just singular like you and I
Maybe try pseudo-Greek like Plattypodes
So we can celebrate him in many odes
What the Victorians missed we could put right
Because the Platypus can't read and write
Or even talk, so he won't shout and cuss
This most puzzling yet singular Platypus

Folliculaphillia

Last year in Mow-Vember my wife for a joke…
Said grow a moustache like that Wolverine bloke
I said to the wife "my dear won't that tickle ya?"
She said "I don't mind, I have Folliculaphillia…"

Folliculaphillia… if you should care
It means she's a woman and she likes facial hair
But a Wolverines 'tache can't be grown in just one day
So I tried different styles as it grew on the way

I tried a Chaplin, a Chevron and a Painter's Brush
A Kaiser, a Dali, a Lampshade and a Walrus
A Fu Manchu, Frank Zappa and Asterix The Gaul
An Albert Einstein, a Jonny Fluffypunk, I tried them all

In films, cartoons and games 'taches steal the show
Captain Haddock, Captain Hook, Luigi and Mario
For some men though proper lip rugs are a mystery
Because they are suffering from mustachular dystrophy

But the Wolverines sideburns, these bits on the side…
Wouldn't grow on my cheeks, believe me I tried…
and I think it's too late for these muscles to grow…
and just look at my fingers my nails hardly show!

So a cautionary tale to all of you folks out there…
you can't become 'The Wolverine' by just growing facial hair
And the reason for this… I think that I found…
Is that Man Makes Moustache not the other way round!

The Poor Man's Friend

Dr Roberts was short in stature he was only five foot high
with a swarthy complexion and a beautiful black eye
his special branded recipe for complaints without end
was simply named and sold as "The Poor Man's Friend"

For his lotions and his potions he charged the going fee
but for many of his patients his advice came for free
His annual publication all about body, mind and health
contained tips conducive to happiness, life and wealth

"The Cottager's Companion", Yes… That was the name
Was sent both far and wide and just added to his fame
But his special branded recipe for complaints without end
was simply named and sold as "The Poor Man's Friend"

Dr Roberts was a Methodist and frequently preached a mass
And his shop was first in Bridport to be fitted with the gas
He experimented with Electricity to help to treat the sick
And cured a man of dumbness with shocks to his neck

He wired up his window to keep rude boys from his shop
It gave a shock to a clients dog so this he vowed to stop
But his special branded recipe for complaints without end
was simply named and sold as "The Poor Man's Friend"

Dr Roberts was a surgeon, apothecary and physician
So he took two apprentices to help him on his mission
and so it was upon his death he passed the business on
to two young men, apothecaries… to Thomas and to John

and so their names were added to the potions outer pot
lettered blue as 'Prepared only by Beach and Barnicott'
Dr Roberts special recipe for complaints without end
simply named and sold as "The Poor Man's Friend"

Medicine for what ails you

Linctus and tinctures, bottles on the shelf

There's blue ones and brown ones

To boost and aid your health

Eczema, scarlatina, typhus, fever ague

Scorbutic eruptions, boils and pimples too

Dysentery, diptheria, scrofula or hooping cough

Whatever your malady we will send you off

With one of our concoctions labelled just for you

But don't ask what's in the jar the ingredients could be poo

You think that I am joking, messing with your head

Try some salts of mercury mixed with venetian red

For abscesses, pustules and for inflammations

Try our bismuth and honey rubbing embrocations

Or rose oil and beeswax for trembling of the heart

Or mustard seeds with turpentine sure to make you fart

Our notions and our lotions if you have the wealth

Are guaranteed to affect your quickly failing health

See us for your ailments or just that little cough

Because whatever your malady we will send you off

Stop Taking The Tabloids

My anxiety is rising… my stress is off the scale

I glimpsed a bloody headline in the Daily Mail

They fill you up with crazy and make your mind obsess

We should waterboard our MPs and make them all confess

Leaning left, leaning right, then they're on the fence

Scrap the trident, ban the bomb, spend more on defence

The security forces watch you with your own webcam

Phishing, skimming, hacking the latest techno scam

Why did they put those masts in the centre of our towns?

Wireless from our smart phones is used to dumb us down!

The rich are getting richer they are standing on our backs

The poor are sponging off the state according to the hacks

The foreigners are coming they're going to take your job

The criminals are outsourcing… to the Russian mob

The food we're eating will kill us it's gone beyond a joke

If you believe the bloody papers your brain will start to smoke

They say theres no solution, this is freedom of the press

Why do we even listen to this right wing craziness?

Take all those hate filled rags and chuck 'em on the fire…

For without a source of income the barons will expire!

Tiddles The Quantum Cat

You may have heard a tale that folks relate
About a cat in a box in a quantum state
That cat is neither alive or dead when it's hid
You can only make sure when you lift the lid

Now Tiddles the cat was the one whose fate
Had been tied forever into that quantum state
So when his mates came and gave him a shout
He couldn't go because he was neither in nor out

Poor little Tiddles he just wasn't really sure
Who he really was and if he existed any more
Being both dead and alive it seems to me
Means that he is probably just a Zombie

One night each year when the veils are thin
Reality gets twisted and they let the others in
So leave out a box with sweets and stuff like that
In case you need to feed Tiddles the Zombie Cat

And if you are out and about on Halloween Night
And hear a strange noise that gives you a fright
It's probably just Tiddles the Zombie Cat
Knocking over bins or something like that

The Interloper

You can sweep it under the carpet and hope it goes away
You can stuff it in your in-tray and save it for another day
You can lock it in a metal crate and throw away the key
or hide it behind the sofa and hope no one else will see
You could put it in a drawer where no else could find it
Or hide it at the zoo where no one else would mind it
You can ignore it, blank it and send it to Coventry
But the more that you ignore it the bigger it will be
You can categorise and label it but you'd best confront it soon
Because you can't go on living with the Elephant in the Room

Have You Ever Been On Your Own?

"When you have sat in your sacred space
And sent your mind to your special place…
Slowed your thoughts till there's nothing there…
Breathed in and out with clean fresh air...

When you have seen that lake in your minds eye
Full of pain from all those tears that you didn't cry
When you have sat upon that lonely shore
Then and only then, and not at all before...

Then you can say you have been on your own!

And when you return from that mind's recess
You can say out loud with no fear of redress
I have traveled far and I have traveled wide
But the hardest journey was the one inside

...and when I did that... I was on my own!"

Storm Front

Storm clouds in the black leaded sky
Mirror the tension behind my eye
A solitary drop of icy, wind blown rain
Hits my hand with a splashing pain

An advance messenger from the Gods
A prelude to a deluge, of falling rods
Umbrellas go up and we start to run
for shelter until the shower is done

A flash of lightning bisects the rain
then through my eyes into my brain
Eight elephants pass between the crack
until the thunder comes rolling back.

The storm has broken. Sun comes out.
Heraldic blackbird begins to shout
His triumphant song for all to hear
Clouds have lifted the sky is clear

Messages From The Past

Stars kiss the earth of the green and ancient land
Earthworks like ripples around the maiden stand
Stones and barrows crest the hills to greet the sun
Landscape whispers tales of people long since gone
Messages from the past sent by the hands of men
Monuments by the living so the dead can walk again

Beltaine

Jack is on his heels falling back
Fast track flowers are busting buds
Trees in soft focus paused to bloom
The earth is breathing in ready to exhale

Hollow Ways

In cloth of ochre the trees stand sway
Beside the hidden ancient way
A sunken path from days of old
Cut from the earth in blocks of gold
This secret place before too long
Will swell with the voice of evensong
As Nature calls her children home
From their quest for food where're they roam
This change of guard at fading light
Is done this way by Nature's rite
And creatures of the night hold sway
Till comes the light at break of day

The Greenwood Tree

Early one April morning
I met a minstrel by the way
He sang as the want of his calling
And this is what he did say

"I met my love 'neath the greenwood tree
When the snow lay on the ground
She said she would be true to me
So we tied the ribbons 'round

Beneath that spreading old yew tree
Our hearts were joined as one
Before the winters numbered three
She gave to me my son

Twelve years soon whistled past
He'd grown up big and strong
A youth so blithe, lithe and fast
He could surely do no wrong

When the Duke he came to town
With his ranks of brave and free
My boy stood up to be a man
To show what he could be

My love, she begged him not to go
For to keep our boy from harm
But a soldier's life she had to know
Was more lively than the farm

And so it was he found his way
With Monmouth and his men
He marched away upon that day
He'd ne'er see Lyme again

At Sedgemoor battle was joined
Under cover of the night
But the farmers boys and free men
Were the losers in the fight

Our boys were forced to kneel and yield
At the hand of King James's Knight
They were taken from the battlefield
And locked up out of sight

Court was brought from out of town
Lord Jeffreys and his advisors
He sat in judgement in his gown
The hanging Judge at the Assizes

And so it was that judgement passed
On the rebellion's sons and daughters
Leaving families to stand aghast
They were hung and drawn in quarters

So I swore an oath to my grieving wife
As long as I drew breath
I'd do all I could to take the life
Of Jeffreys who'd brought such death

I dogged his heels for three long year
Taking work where ere it led
Serving rumour with his wine and beer
To get inside his head

Whispers made to listening ears
And chalk on his window ledge
Were all I needed to feed his fears
And put Jeffreys right on edge

Fortunes changed and the king he fled
To his people out in France
King William and Mary ruled instead
And here I found my chance

Jeffreys saw the wind of change
He knew what he had to do
So as quickly as he could arrange
Like James… Jeffreys fled too

When Jeffreys ran he was in disguise
Dressed as a common sailor
So I bought a man who could recognise
The butcher in his regalia

Jeffreys hid and went to ground
But was caught in a Ramsgate pub
He thought it safe the place he found
But my coins had bought his blood

Jeffreys as a man was most reviled
By commoner and lord alike
He was held in the tower in some style
To keep his head from off a pike

My next job was as his jailor
In the dankest London Tower
His food and drink my favour
And thus I found my power

So it was that Jeffreys ailed
From poisons slipped by me
He wept with pain, his kidneys failed
and then he died in agony

Now I return to that greenwood tree
and my lovely maiden fair
I hope that she still waits for me
With a ribbon in her hair"

Indigo

Held in the cradling coils of a scented heaven
Blown to the mind shore by a startled zephyr
Kissed on the lips by a hint of apple blossom
Loved last night by your lingering presence

Give me a T…

I know I don't always say
That I love you every day
But between you and me
There is this ritual of tea
And I can say with Darjeeling
Somethings about my feeling
This 'tea ritual' that we do
Says "I will always love you"

Factor in the Tractor

In Dorsetshire we've got it all
The landscape and attractions
For adults to children small
We have the best distractions

Our little lanes and scenic views
Are the best beyond reproach
But satnavs driving time it skews
When you're stuck behind a coach

If you live your life at the speed of light
Then Dorset's not for you
But if you feel our pace of life is right
Then here's what you should do

Factor in the Tractor
If you're on the road, on your way
Factor in the Tractor
Because we don't have motorway

Is It Too Late To Be Writing Poetry?

I'm tired and I just can't stop yawning
It's stupid o'clock in the bloody morning
We will just have to wait and see
If it's too late to be writing poetry?
I really need some divine intervention
perhaps an elixir of lyrical inspiration
I drifted and snoozed and finally slumped
and only woke when my head got bumped!
Perhaps a surgeon would do instead
To remove this keyboard from my head

Parrot Cat

Parrot Cat, Paraquat
You are like a poison to me
You get inside my defences
You show me how to be
A little bit fluffy round the edges
And fierce when I need to be
But I have to stop eating mice
They don't agree with me!

What Did You Do In The War?

I was a clicktavist on the font line
when the politicians scammed the people
and the tyrants screamed 'fake news'
I was there when we built the machines
that rolled into peoples homes
distracting them with cats and puppies
I was there when we trained the captains of industry
that steered our financial systems onto the rocks
I was one of the dealers that enabled the addicts
to get streaming media and access to celebrity culture

I apologise unreservedly for my part
in the dissemination of early memes
I beg your forgiveness for the damage to the environment
caused by the throwaway technology that we created
I am sorry for my role in releasing the billion headed hydra
that hijacked the world wide web scatting spam and deceit
and releasing troll armies on an unsuspecting population

So... What did I do in the war?

I trained the people who are fighting back
against the relentless tide of stultifying stupidity
I am opening people's eyes to prevent
blind obedience to the corporate message
I am shouting my truth from every platform
and every technological device at my disposal

So... What are you doing in the war?